ISAAC NEWTON

THE SMARTEST PERSON THAT EVER LIVED

Biography of Famous People Grade 3 | Children's Biography Books

BABY PROFESSOR
EDUCATION KIDS

Speedy Publishing LLC

40 E. Main St. #1156

Newark, DE 19711

www.speedypublishing.com

Copyright 2017

All Rights reserved. No part of this book may be reproduced or used in any way or form or by any means whether electronic or mechanical, this means that you cannot record or photocopy any material ideas or tips that are provided in this book

Isaac Newton was known to be one of the greatest scientists in history. Albert Einstein even made the comment that Newton was the smartest person that had ever lived.

Sir Isaac Newton

Newton developed the laws of motion (which proceeded to become the basis for physics), the theory of gravity, calculus, as well as making breakthroughs in areas of optics, including the reflecting telescope. Read further to learn more about this amazing astronomer, mathematician and scientist.

Sir Isaac Newton

Woolsthorpe, England

HIS EARLY YEARS

Newton was born on January 4, 1643 in Woolsthorpe, England. His father was a farmer who was named Isaac Newton as well. He died three months before the birth of his son. His mother then remarried when Isaac was three and left him to be cared for by his grandparents.

He attended school and was considered an adequate student. His mother tried to remove him from school at one point to help with the farm, but young Isaac did not care for this idea and soon returned to school.

The Kings School

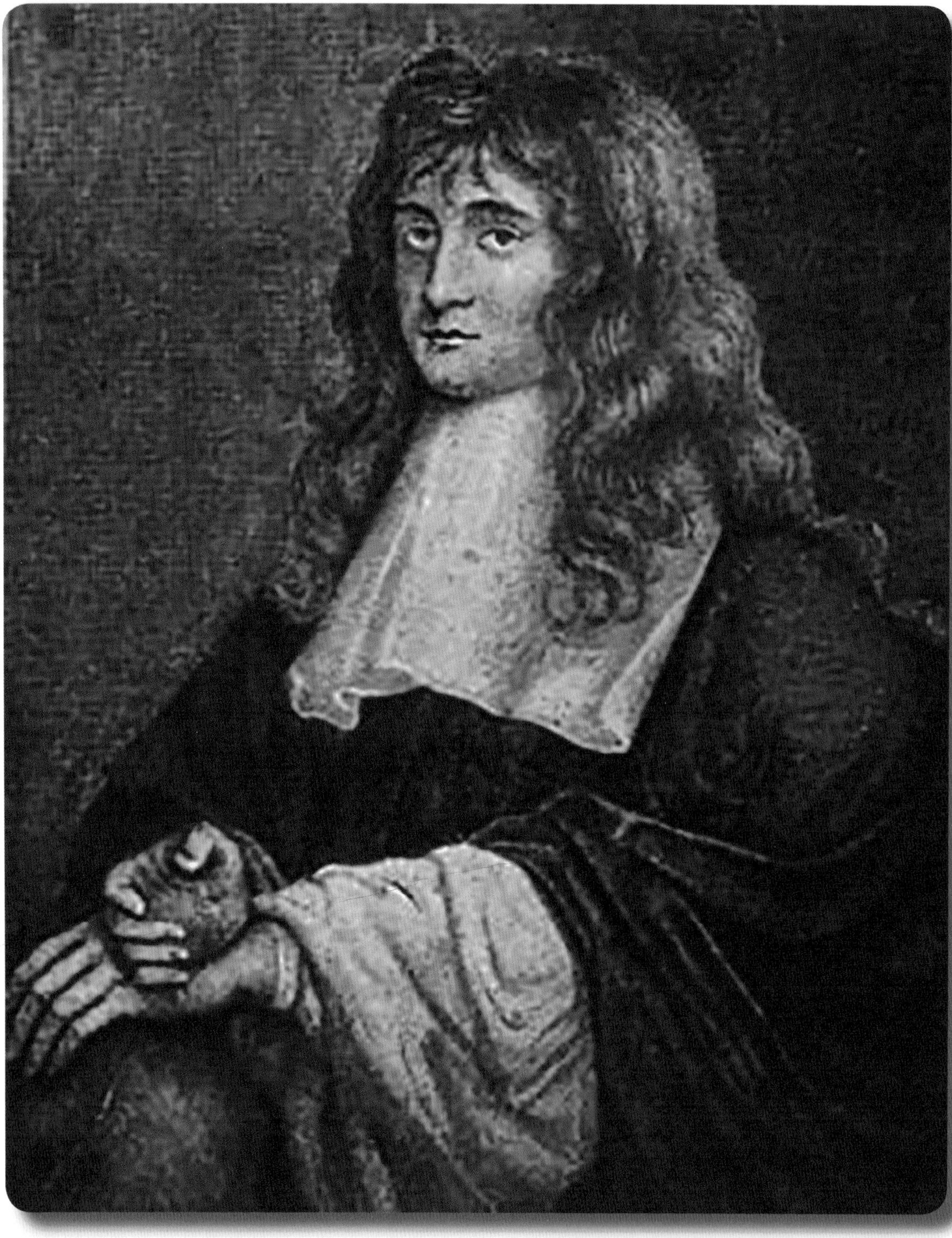

Isaac basically grew up alone. During the rest of his life, he preferred to live and work alone, focusing on his studies and writings.

NEWTON'S COLLEGE AND CAREER

He read and studied about classic astronomers and philosophers including Galileo, Rene Descartes, Johannes Kepler, Copernicus and Aristotle.

Galileo Galilei studying a globe

Statue of Isaac Newton at Cambridge

Isaac started college at Cambridge in 1661. He spent most of his life there as he became a professor of mathematics as well as a fellow of the Royal Society, which was a group of scientists in England. Eventually, he became elected to represent Cambridge as a member of parliament.

From 1665 to 1667 he had to leave the University due to the Great Plague. He would spend these two years in isolation, studying at home in Woolsthrope, working on his theories on the laws of motion, gravity and calculus.

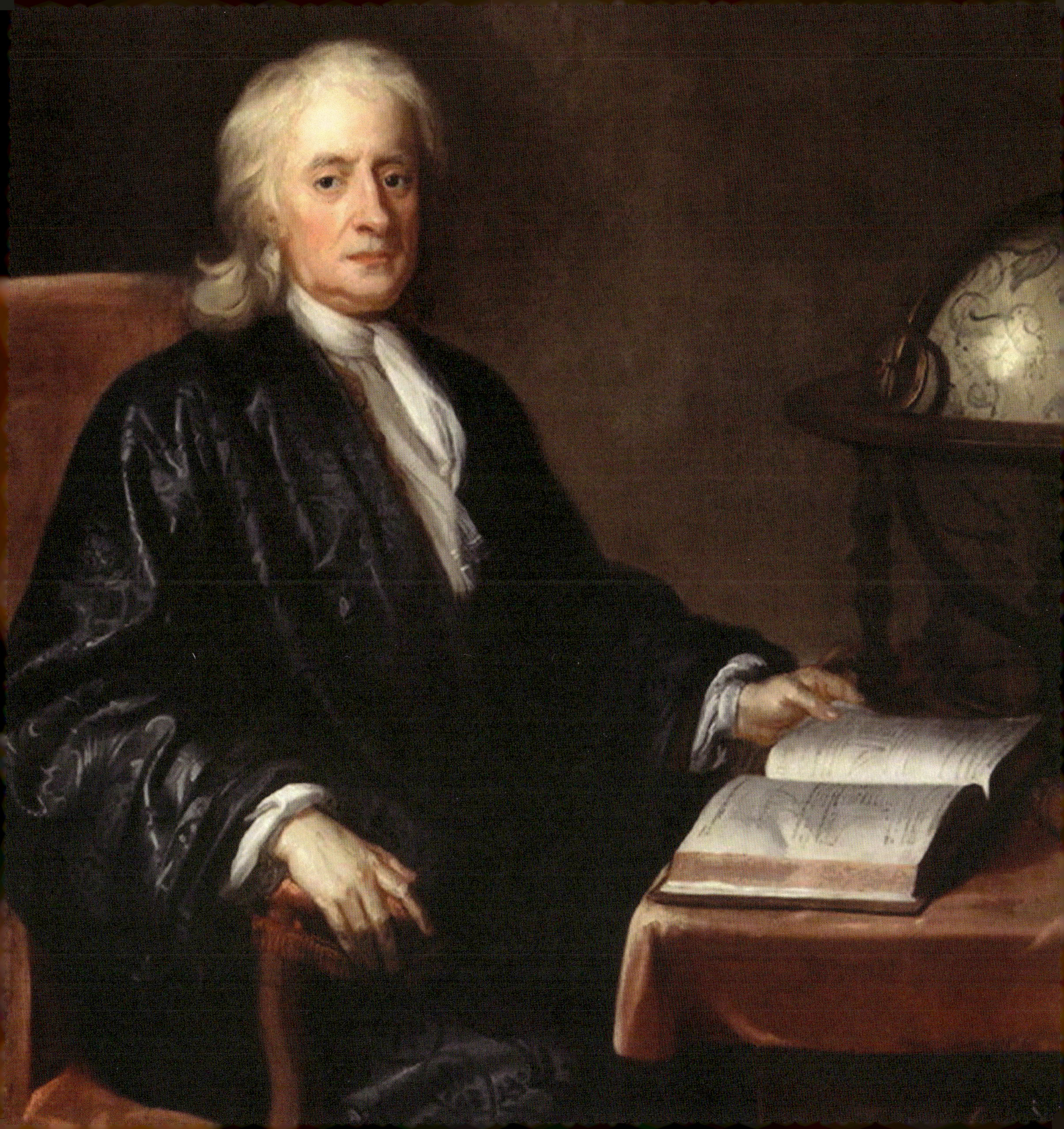

Royal Mint Building

Newton became warden to the Royal Mint in London in 1996. He was very serious about his duties and tried to rid England of corruption as well as reforming its currency. In 1703 he was elected as President of the Royal Society and Queen Anne knighted him in 1705.

THE PRINCIPIA

Newton proceeded to publish his most significant work named the Philosophiae Naturalis Principia Mathematica (meaning "Mathematical Principals of Natural Philosophy") in 1687. In this writing, he defined the three laws of motion and the law of universal gravity. The work would proceed to go down in history as one of the most significant works in science. Not only did it introduce the gravity theory, but also identified the principles of modern physics.

PHILOSOPHIÆ
NATURALIS
PRINCIPIA
MATHEMATICA.

Autore *JS. NEWTON,* Trin. Coll. Cantab. Soc. Matheseos
Professore *Lucasiano,* & Societatis Regalis Sodali.

IMPRIMATUR·
S. PEPYS, *Reg. Soc.* PRÆSES.
Julii 5. 1686.

LONDINI,

Jussu *Societatis Regiæ* ac Typis *Josephi Streater.* Prostat apud
plures Bibliopolas. Anno MDCLXXXVII.

Albert Einstein

GRAVITY

Newton was the first scientist to describe gravity mathematically. This was known as Newton's Law of University Gravitation. Albert Einstein would make improvements to this theory in his theory of relativity.

The strange force that makes an object fall towards the Earth is known as gravity. As it turn outs, all objects experience gravity. However, there are some objects, like the Sun and the Earth, that have considerably more gravity than other objects. The size of the object determines how much gravity it has, or, the volume of its mass. It is also dependent upon how close the object is to you. The closer you are to the object, the greater the gravitational pull.

$$F_1 = F_2 = G\frac{m_1 \times m_2}{r^2}$$

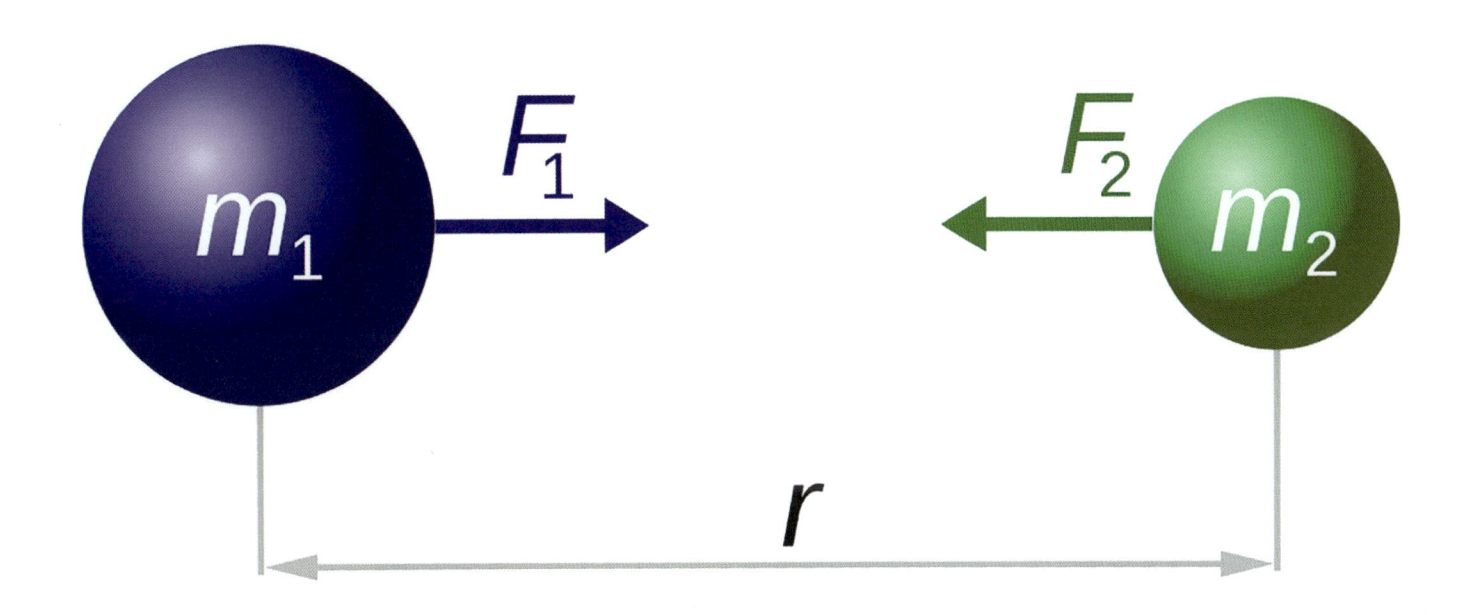

Newtons Law of Universal Gravitation

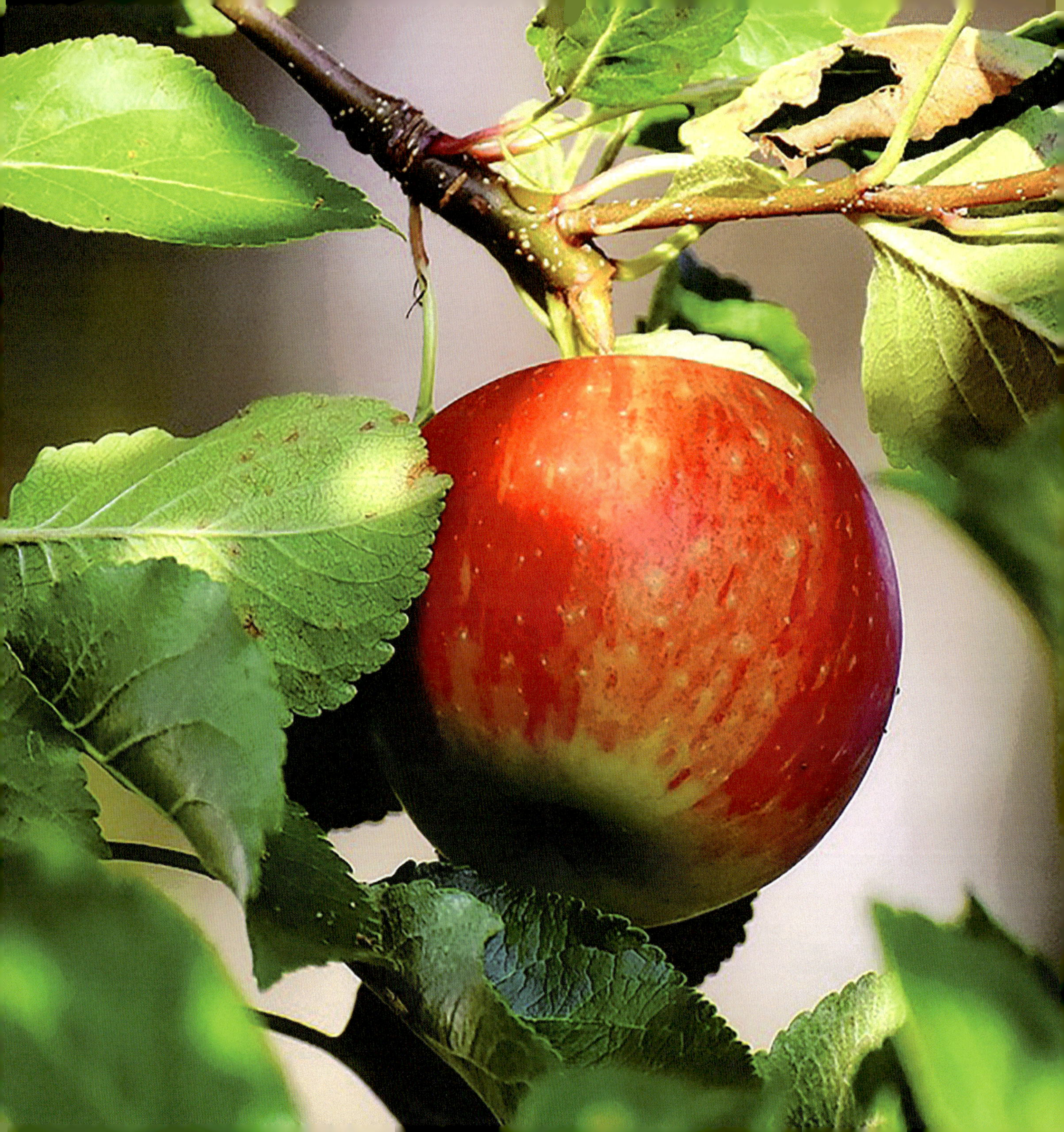

It is said that he got this gravity idea on the farm, when he observed an apple falling from a tree.

LAWS OF MOTION

Newton came up with these laws so he could scientifically describe how objects move.

Isaac Newton showing an experiment

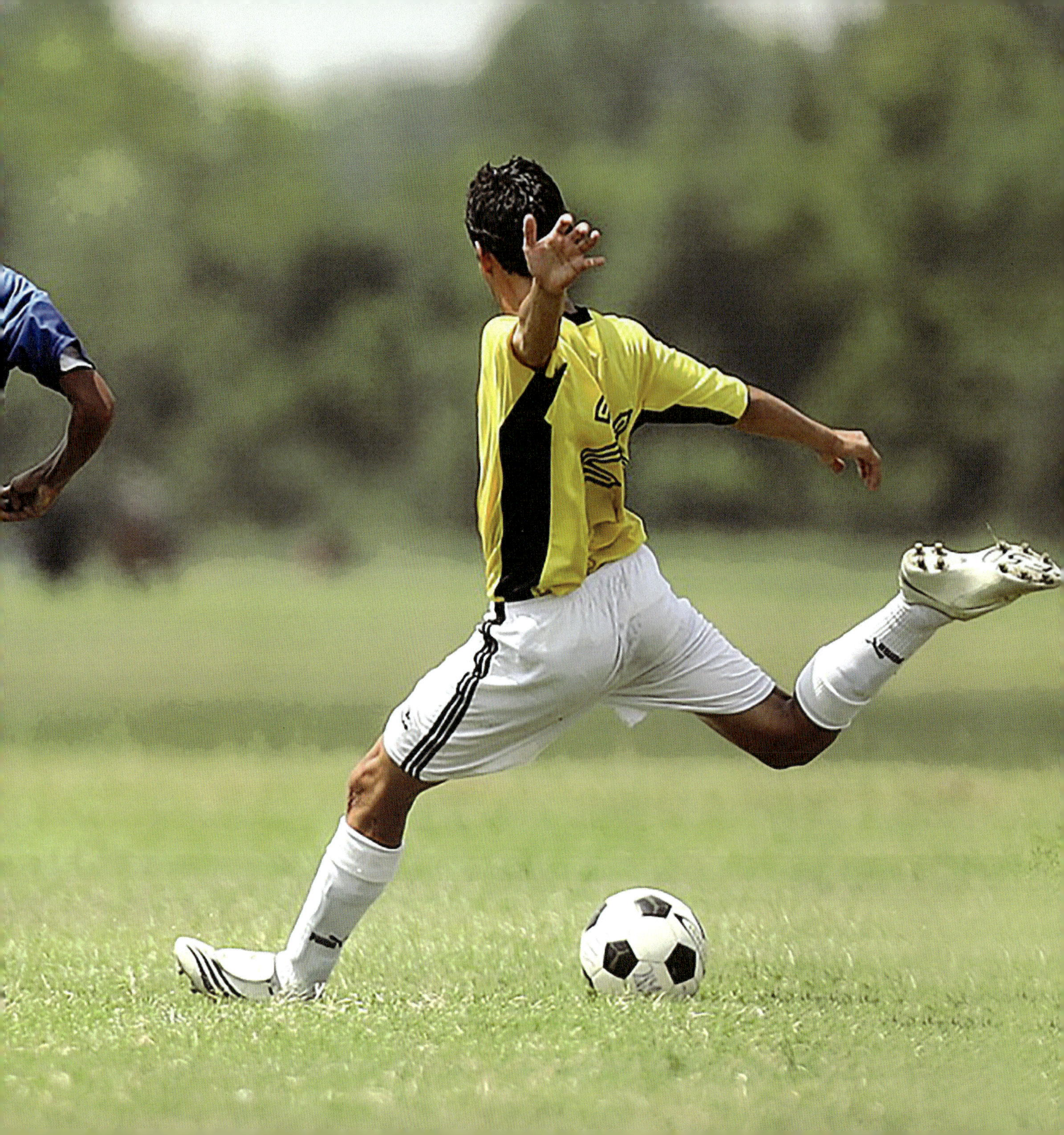

Anything that changes the state of motion of an object is known as a force. You use force as you push a letter on the keyboard or when kicking a ball. Forces are all around you. Gravity acts as a continuous force on your person, and keeps you secure on Earth so that you do not fall off.

When describing force, we use strength and direction. An example would be as you kick a ball, you exert force in an exact direction. That would be the direction that you want the ball to travel. In addition, the harder you kick it, the more force you put on it, and the farther the ball will go.

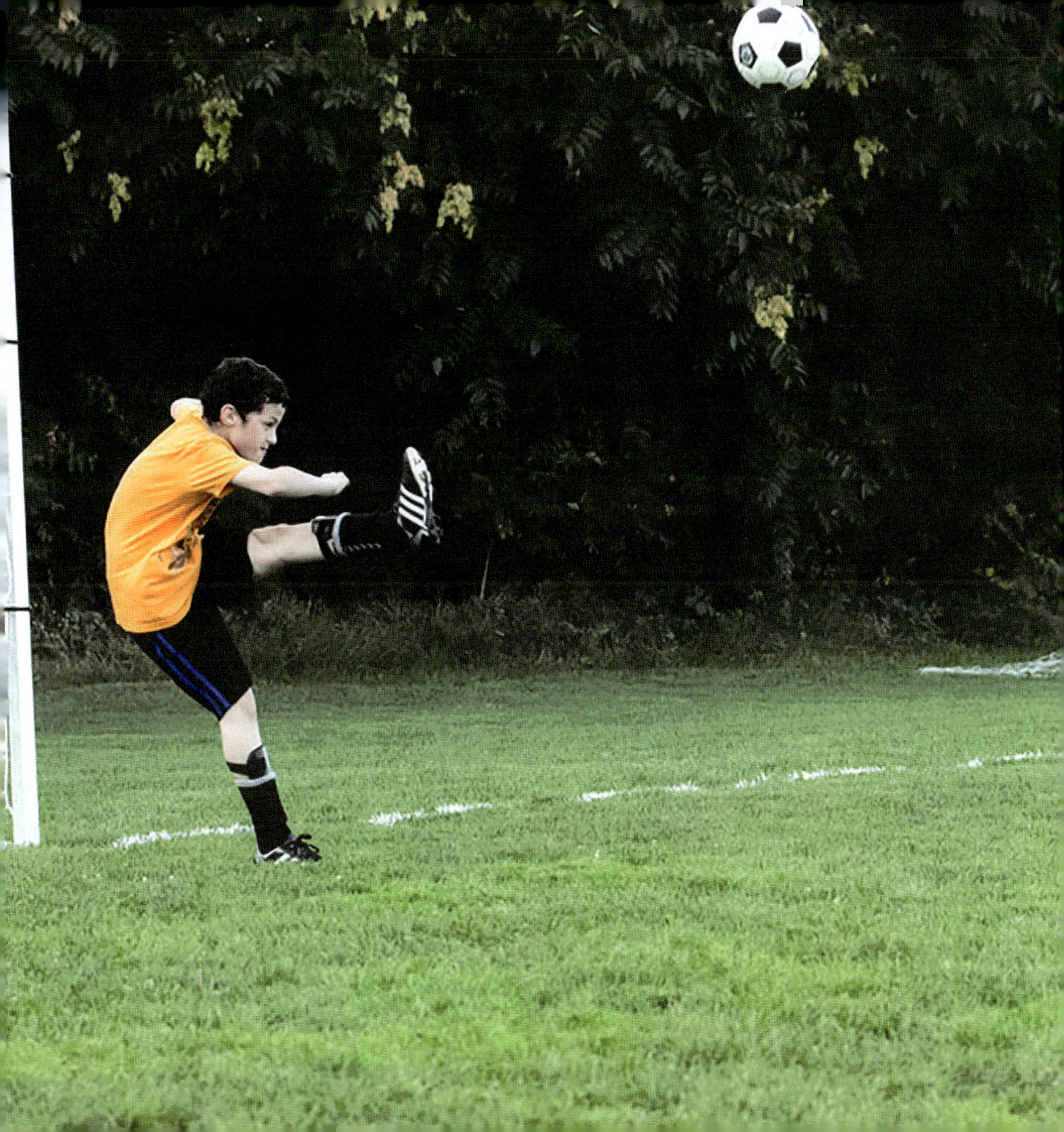

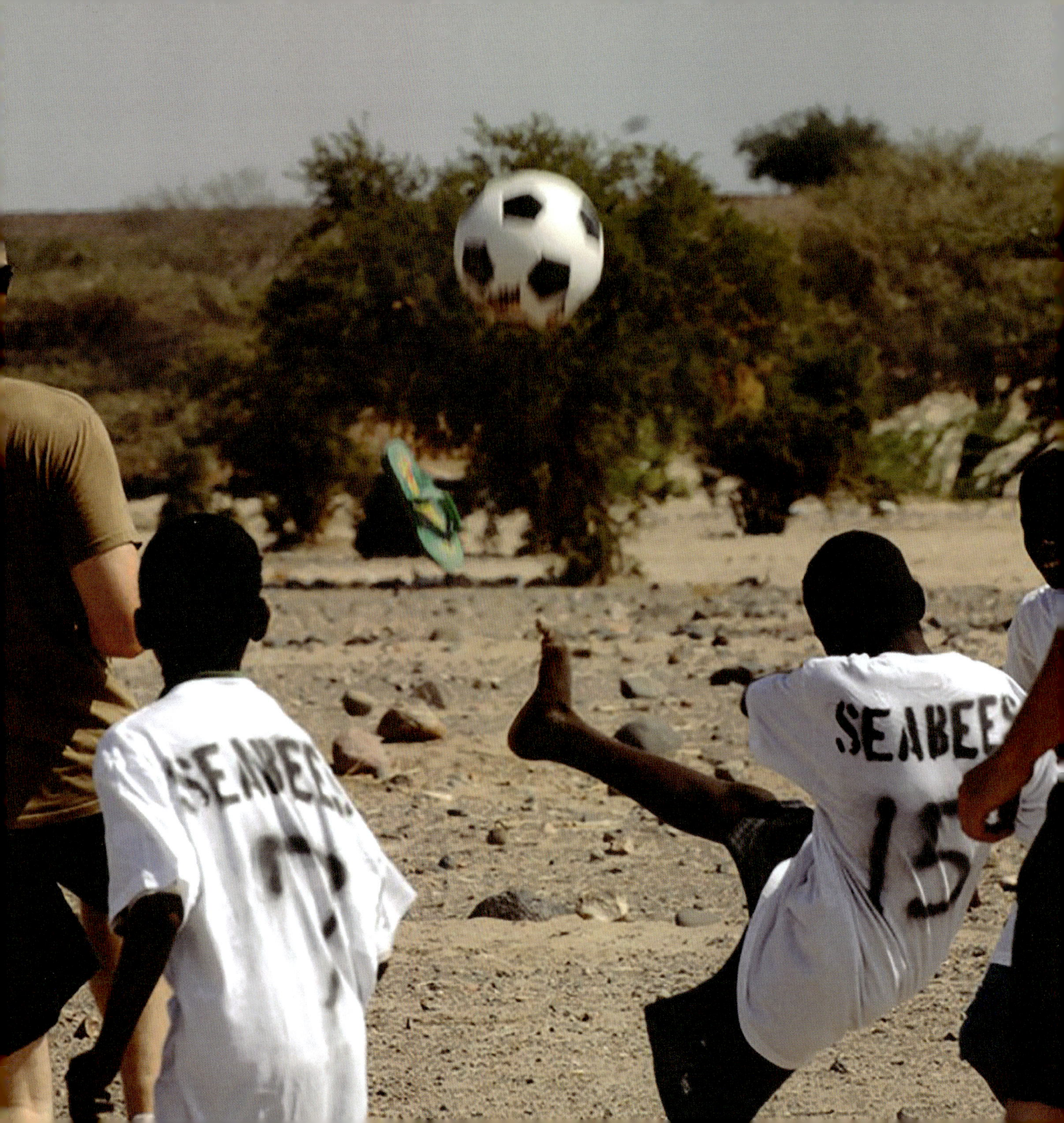
SEABEES
SEABEES
15

THE FIRST LAW OF MOTION

The first law indicates that any item in motion continues to move at the same speed and in the same direction, unless other forces act to change it. What this means is that when you kick the ball it will fly forever until some other force acts on it. While this may sound strange, it is very true. Once you kick it, forces begin acting on it immediately. These forces include friction or air resistance and the gravitational pull. Gravity will pull the ball down to the ground and air resistance causes it to slow down.

THE SECOND LAW OF MOTION

The second law indicates that the stronger the object's mass, the more force it takes for acceleration of the object. This is the equation: Force = mass x acceleration or $F = ma$. This means also that the more force you use when kicking the ball, the farther distance it will travel. While, this seems obvious to us, scientists find having an equation for figuring the math and science quite helpful.

Isaac Newton Institute Building

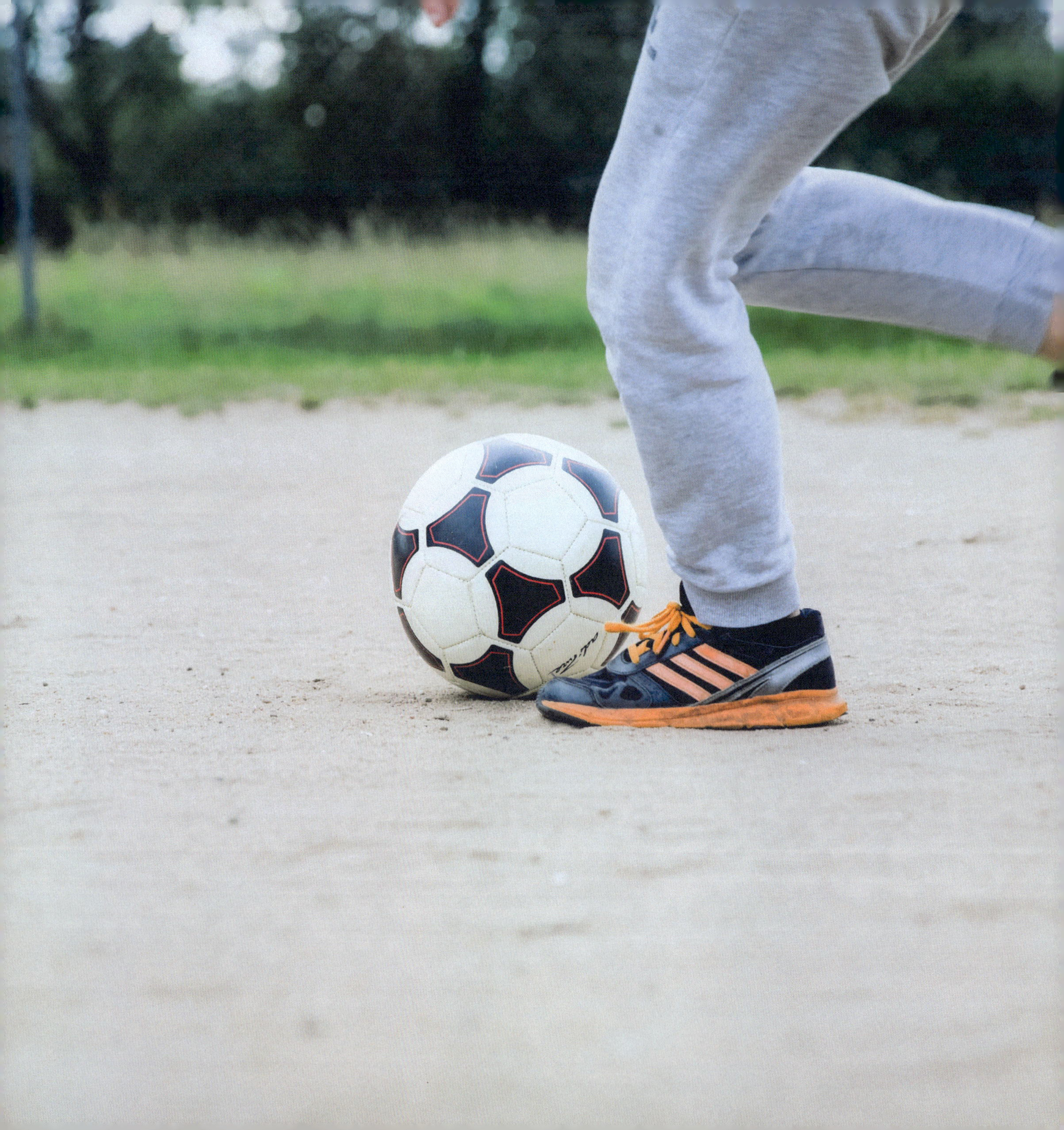

THE THIRD LAW OF MOTION

The third law indicates that for each action, there will be an equal and opposite reaction. What this means is that there will always be two similar forces. In the example used above where you kicked a ball, there is force from your foot to the ball, as well as the same force that is placed by the ball onto your foot, taking place in the opposite direction.

THE REFLECTING TELESCOPE

The reflecting telescope was invented by Isaac Newton in 1668. He used a concave primary mirror along with a flat diagonal secondary mirror. Most of the telescopes used in astronomy today are reflecting telescopes. The reflecting telescope causes the image to reflect to a focus point using mirrors.

Reflecting Telescope

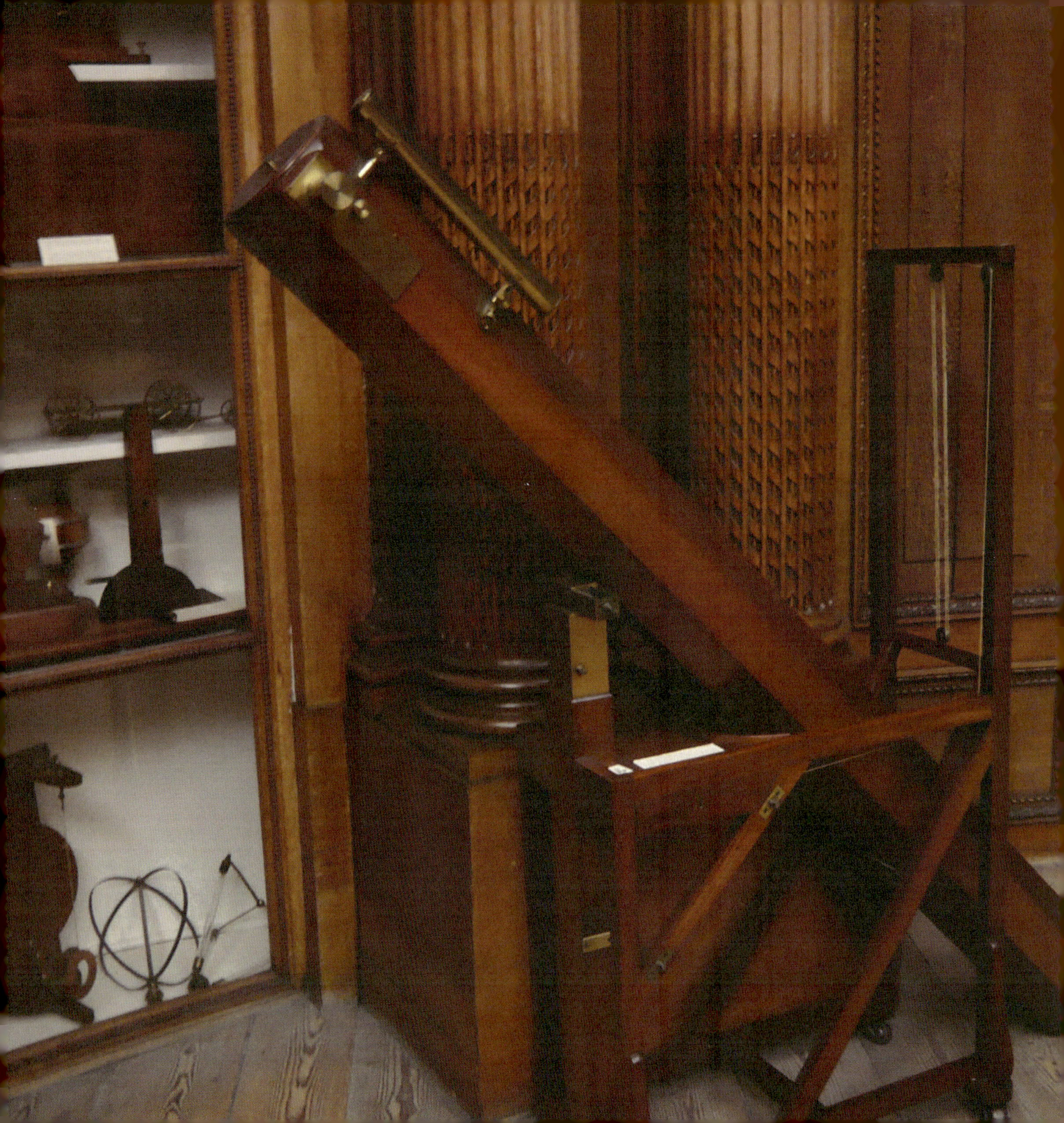

The main advantage of the reflector telescope is that they do not suffer from chromatic aberration since the wavelengths will all reflect off of the mirror in the exact same way. This was a tremendous problem with the refractor telescope. Chromatic aberration is a common optical problem occurring when one lens is unable to bring the wavelengths of color to the same focal plane, or when the color wavelengths become focused at various positions.

Since all wavelengths reflect off of the mirror the same way, reflector telescopes will not experience chromatic aberration, and the result will be a clearer picture. Reflector telescopes are also cheaper to make than the refactor telescopes of the same size.

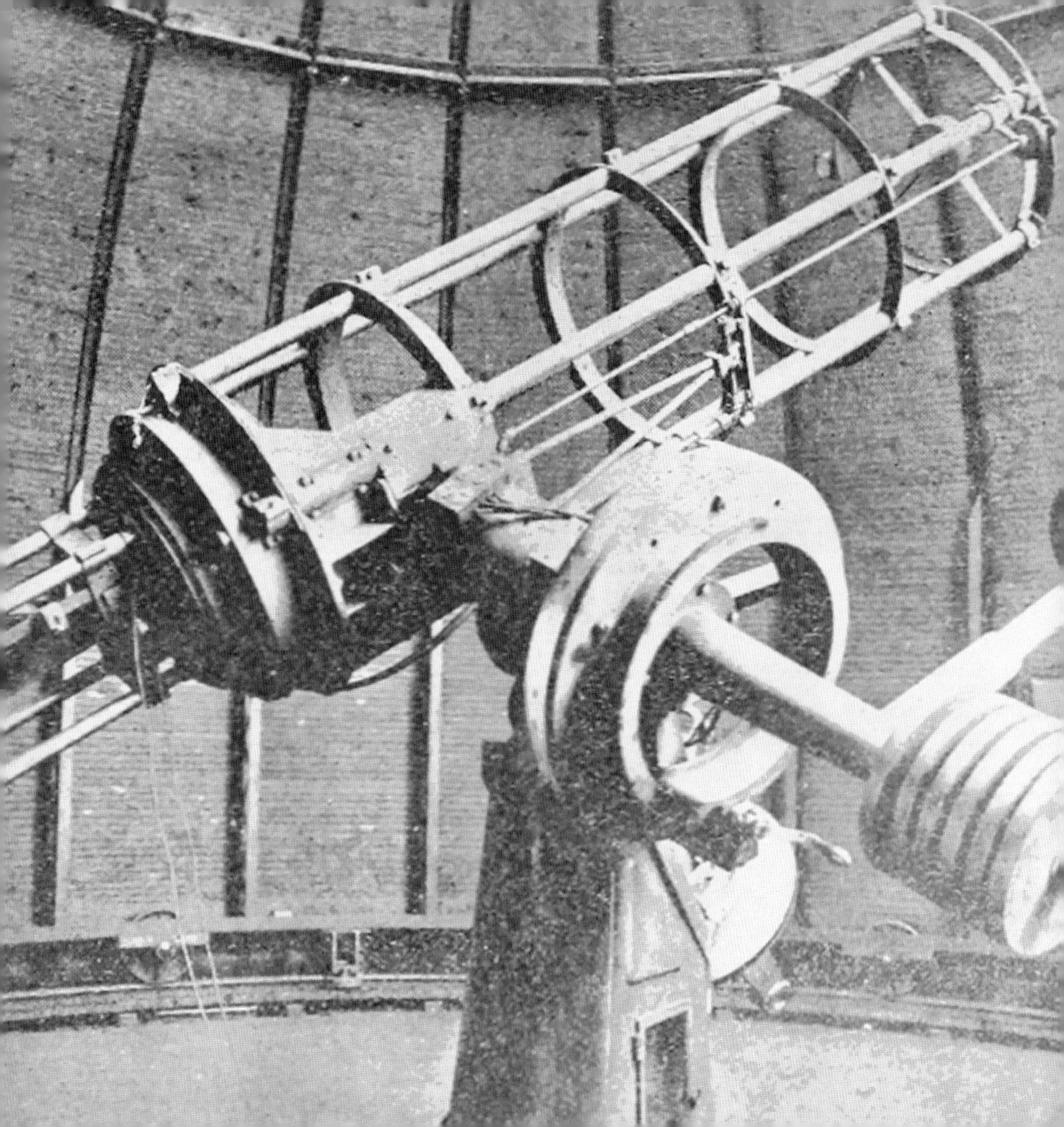

LA MÉTHODE DES FLUXIONS,

ET DES SUITES INFINIES.

Par M. le Chevalier NEWTON.

Traduite par Buffon.

Saw this book for the first time May 7, 1852.
led to it by Dr Jas Wilson's answer to part of
the preface.
                                    A. DeMorgan

A PARIS,

Chez DE BURE l'aîné, Libraire, Quay des Augustins, à Saint Paul.

M. DCC. XL.

Book of Fluxions

CALCULUS

Newton invented "fluxions", a new version of mathematics. Today, it is known as math calculus and is used in science and advanced engineering.

It is a branch of mathematics, and developed from geometry and algebra. Its main focus is on rates of change, within functions, including slopes, curves and accelerations.

THE
METHOD of FLUXIONS
AND
INFINITE SERIES;
WITH ITS

Application to the Geometry of CURVE-LINES.

By the INVENTOR
Sir ISAAC NEWTON, K[t].
Late President of the Royal Society.

Translated from the AUTHOR's LATIN ORIGINAL
not yet made publick.

To which is subjoin'd,

A PERPETUAL COMMENT upon the whole Work,

Consisting of

ANNOTATIONS, ILLUSTRATIONS, and SUPPLEMENTS,

In order to make this Treatise

A compleat Institution for the use of LEARNERS.

By *JOHN COLSON*, M.A. and F.R.S.
Master of Sir *Joseph Williamson*'s free Mathematical-School at *Rochester*.

LONDON:
Printed by HENRY WOODFALL;
And Sold by JOHN NOURSE, at the *Lamb* without *Temple-Bar.*
M.DCC.XXXVI.

Voltaire

HIS PERSONAL LIFE

While it had been claimed that he had been engaged at one time, he was never married. Voltaire, a French writer and philosopher, at the time of Isaac's funeral, made the statement that he "was never sensible to any passion, was not subject to the common frailties of mankind, nor had any commerce with women – a circumstance which was assured me by the physician and surgeon who attended him in his last moments".

Newton was close with Nicolas Fatio de Duillier, a Swiss mathematician, who he had met in London sometime around 1690. In 1693, this intense friendship came to an unexplained and abrupt ending. Newton had a nervous breakdown at the same time. In September of that same year, Newton began sending crazy accusatory letters to friends John Locke and Samuel Pepys. In his note to Locke, he wrote that Locke "endeavored to embroil me with women".

Nicolas Fatio de Duillier

Isaac Newton Monument

NEWTON'S LEGACY

Sir Isaac Newton passed away in London, England on March 31, 1727 as one of the greatest scientists in history, alongside greats such as Galileo, Aristotle and Albert Einstein.

His monument can be viewed in Westminster Abbey, near his tomb. It was created by sculptor Michael Rysbrack in grey and white marble with a design by architect William Kent. It features a figure of Isaac reclining at the top of a sarcophagus, with his right elbow placed on many of his great books and his left hand pointing at a scroll that contains a mathematical design. There is a pyramid with a celestial globe above him that shows the Zodiac signs and the 1680 comet path. There is a relief panel depicting putti using such instruments as the prism and the telescope.

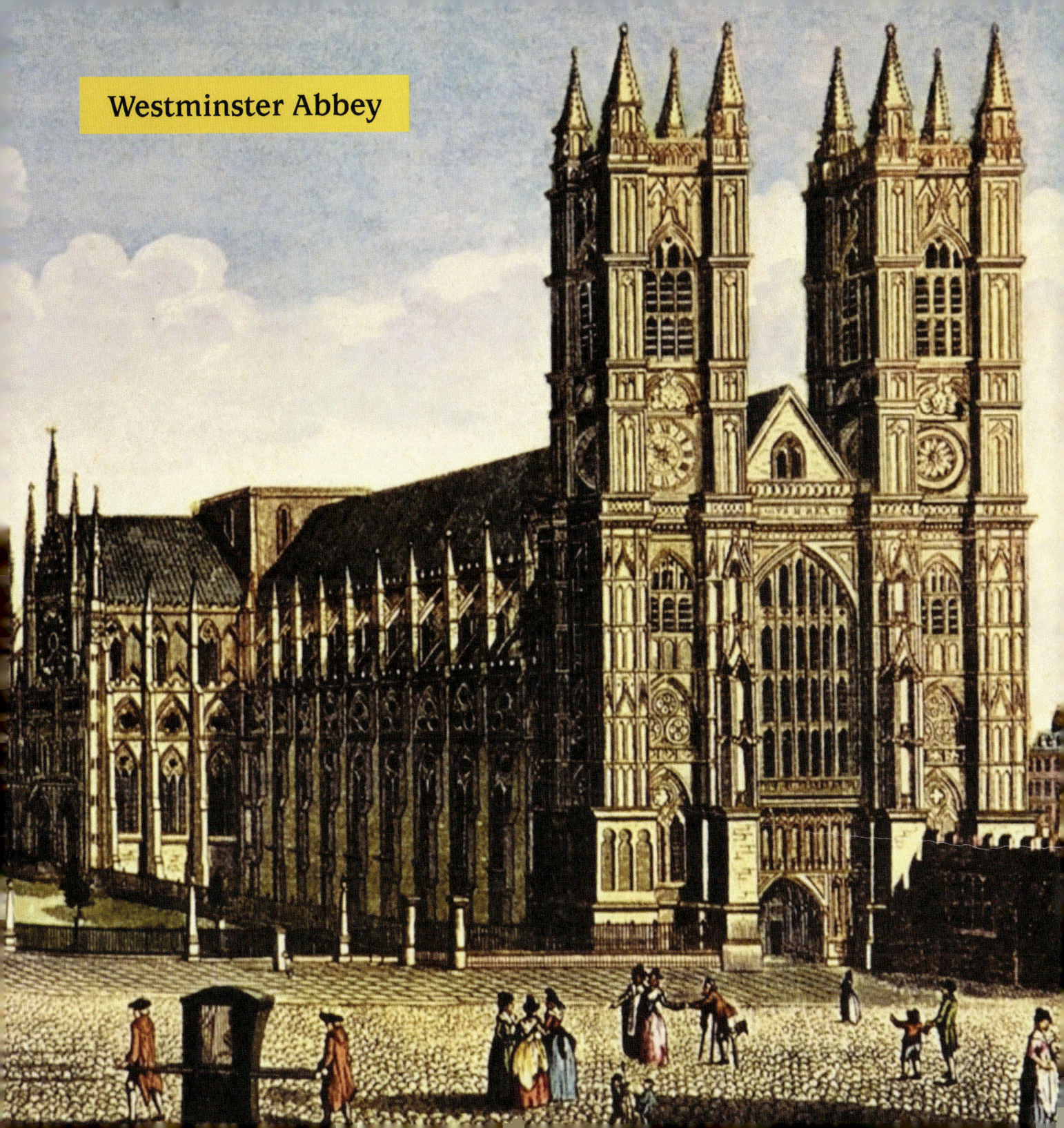

Westminster Abbey

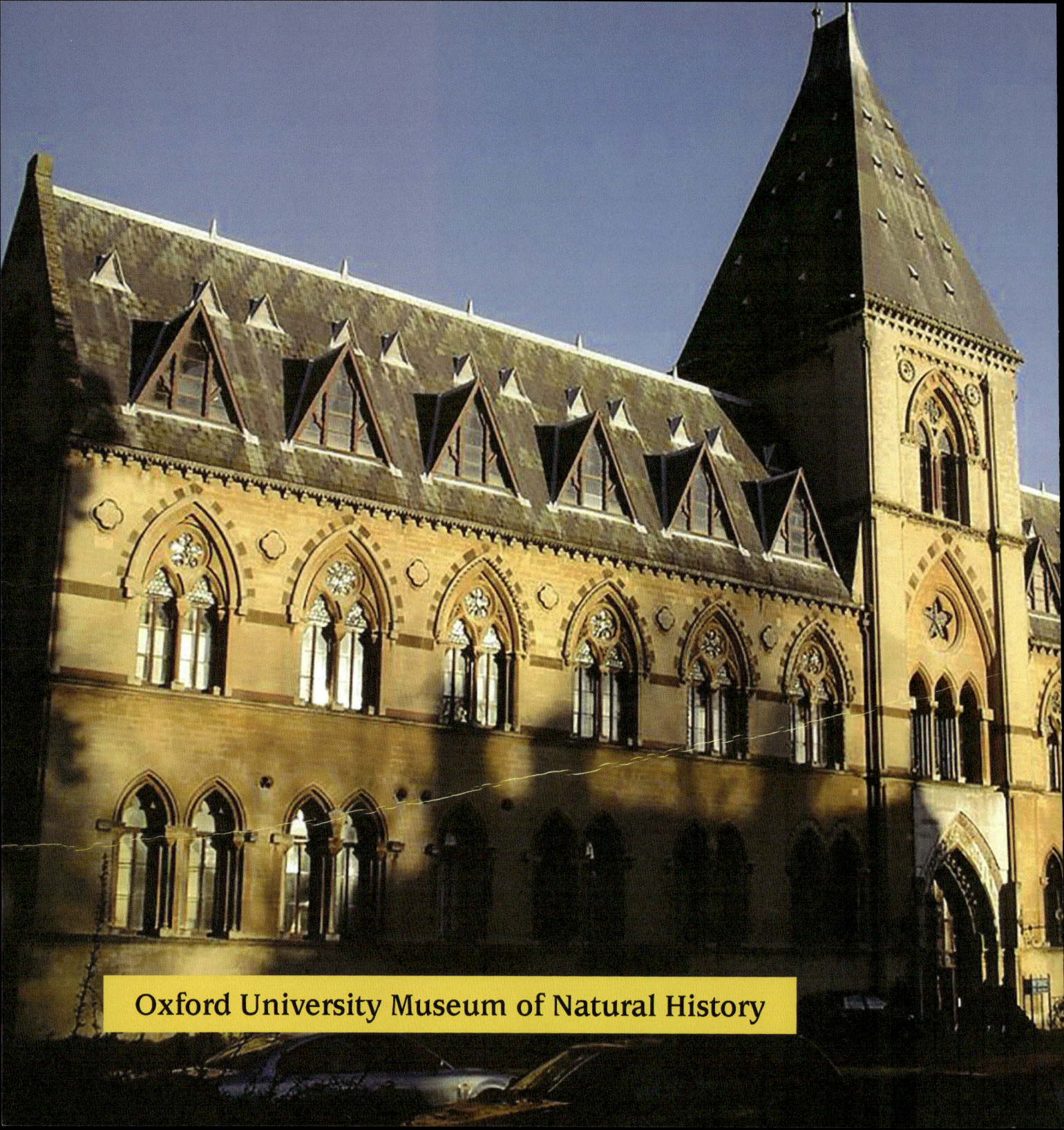

Oxford University Museum of Natural History

There is also a statue of him at the Oxford University Museum of Natural History, where he is seen looking towards an apple located at his feet.

For additional information about Sir Isaac Newton and his discoveries, you can go to your local library, research the internet and ask questions of your teachers, family and friends.

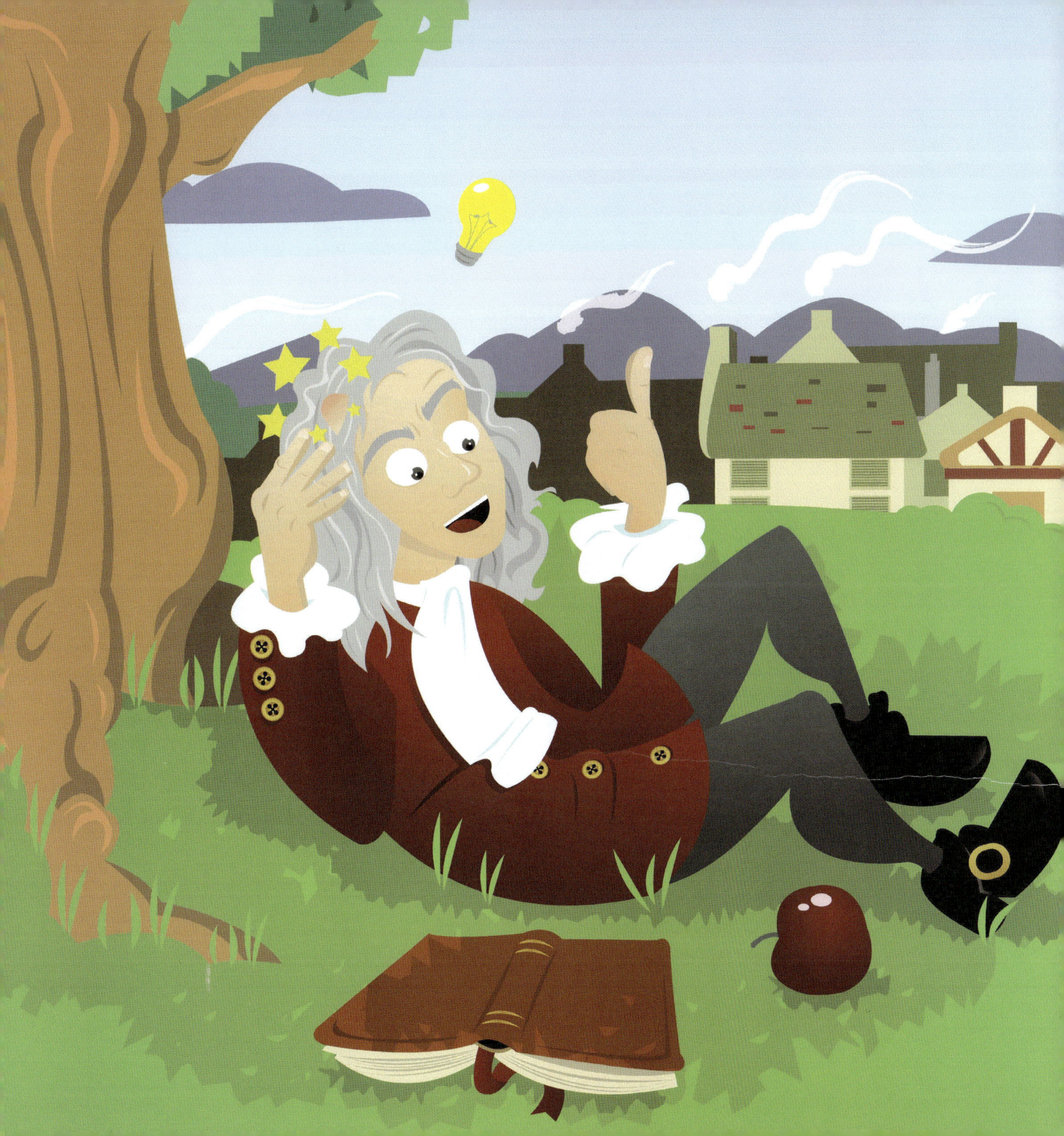

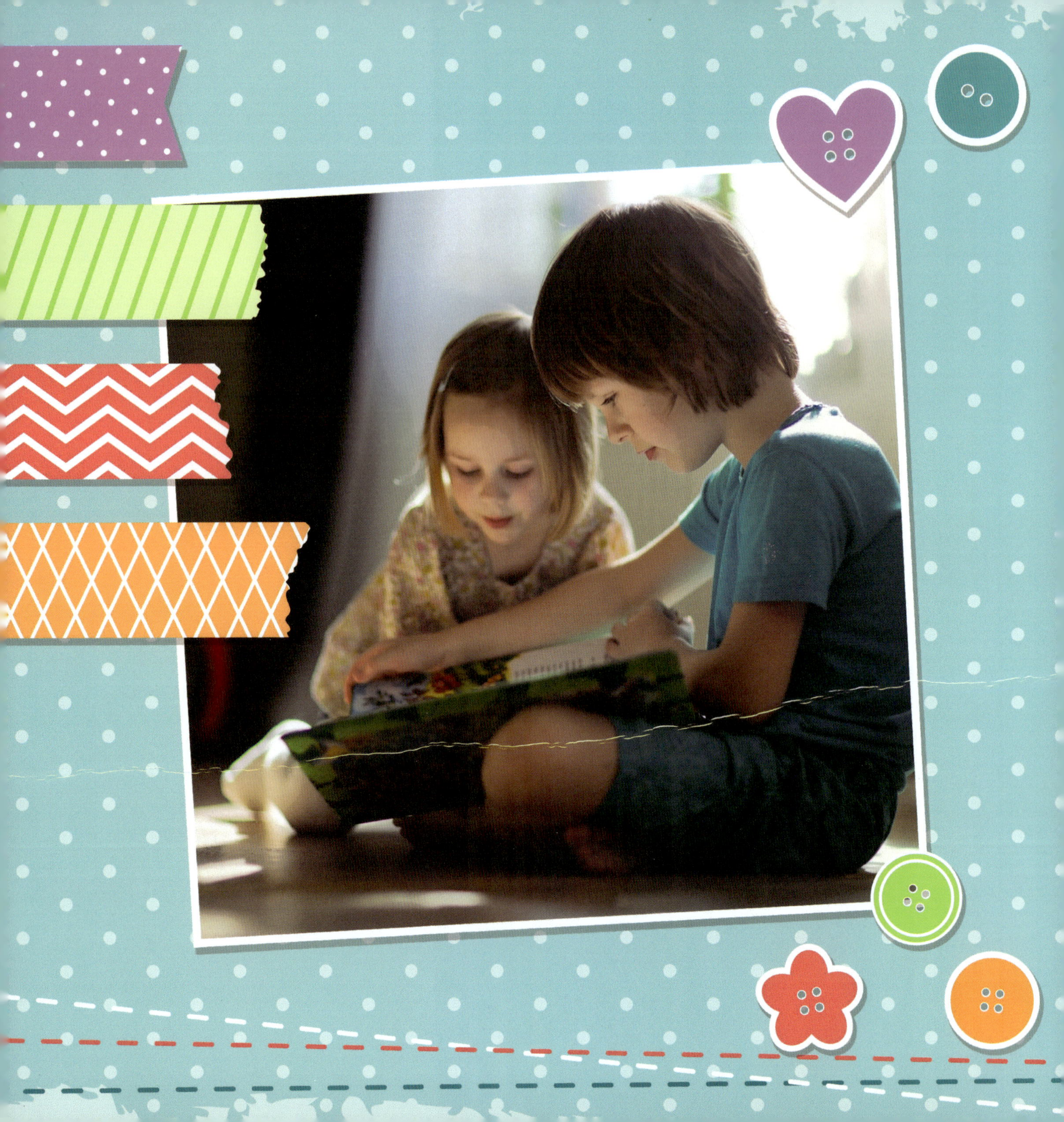

Visit

BABY PROFESSOR
EDUCATION KIDS

www.BabyProfessorBooks.com

to download Free Baby Professor eBooks and view our catalog of new and exciting Children's Books

Printed in Great Britain
by Amazon